D1366459

What Good Is an O?

amicus readers

1

by Marie Powell

Say Hello to Amicus Readers.

You'll find our helpful dog, Amicus, chasing a ball—to let you know the reading level of a book.

1

Learn to Read

Frequent repetition, high frequency words, and close photo-text matches introduce familiar topics and provide ample support for brand new readers.

2

Read Independently

Some repetition is mixed with varied sentence structures and a select amount of new vocabulary words are introduced with text and photo support.

3

Read to Know More

Interesting facts and engaging art and photos give fluent readers fun books both for reading practice and to learn about new topics.

Amicus Readers are published by Amicus
P.O. Box 1329, Mankato, MN 56002
www.amicuspublishing.us

Library of Congress Cataloging-in-Publication Data

Powell, Marie, 1958-, author.
  What good is an O? / by Marie Powell.
    pages cm. -- (Vowels)
  Summary: "Beginning readers are introduced to the vowel O and its sounds and uses, including the double oo sound."-- Provided by publisher.
  ISBN 978-1-60753-711-3 (library binding)
  ISBN 978-1-60753-815-8 (ebook)
  1. Vowels--Juvenile literature. 2. English language--Vowels--Juvenile literature. I. Title.
  PE1157.P6944 2015
  428.1'3--dc23
                        2014045795

Photo Credits: iStock/Thinkstock, cover, 1, 3; Eric Isselee/Shutterstock Images, 4-5; Dave M. Hunt Photography/Shutterstock Images, 6-7, 16 (top right); Paula French/Shutterstock Images, 9, 16 (bottom right); Tom Reichner/Shutterstock Images, 10, 16 (bottom left); Julie Clopper/Shutterstock Images, 13; Shutterstock Images, 14; Torsten Dietrich/Shutterstock Images, 16 (top left)

Produced for Amicus by The Peterson Publishing Company and Red Line Editorial.

Editor Jenna Gleisner
Designer Craig Hinton

Printed in Malaysia
10 9 8 7 6 5 4 3 2 1

What good is an O? An O
is a vowel, like A, E, I, U,
and Y. What sounds does
O make?

<u>O</u> can have a long sound,
like its name.

<u>O</u>livia sees a g<u>o</u>ld geck<u>o</u>.

<u>O</u> can have a short sound.
T<u>o</u>m sees an <u>o</u>tter in
the p<u>o</u>nd.

O can start a word.
An old ostrich runs over
to the fence.

O can come in the middle of a word. A frog hops on top of a log.

Two <u>O</u>s together make the oo sound. S<u>oo</u>n we will leave the z<u>oo</u> and go back to sch<u>oo</u>l.

O at the end of a word can have the long O or oo sound. Who wants to go see the animals again? We do!

Vowel: O

Which words have a long <u>O</u> sound?

Which words have a short <u>O</u> sound?

gecko

otter

frog

ostrich